CHANNELING the GUIDES and ANGELS of LIGHT

MELANIE BECKLER

CONTENTS

PREFACE

This book presents direct-channeled teachings from the Guides and Angels of the Light.

Alongside every word in the book is an uplifting angelic frequency. As you read, you will be guided to open your heart, shift your perspective within, and feel, experience, see, and know that you are in the presence of angels.

To gain the most benefit from reading, think of this book as reading meditations. Take your time as you read the pages, allowing yourself to enter into a soft, relaxed state of being—as if the angels are in your presence and speaking directly to you... one word at a time. They are!

Angels transcend time and space and can be with everyone who calls upon them at the same time. When you read these words, know that you are in the direct presence of your guides and angels, who lovingly and powerfully assist you in tuning into the love, wisdom, and uplifting frequency available for you now.

INVOCATION

At this time, I ask that we be surrounded with divine white light and with each of our highest, best, most loving possible guides and angels of love, light, and healing who can most serve.

Please come in, lift us in vibration, and assist us in quieting our minds and opening our hearts to tune in to knowledge, wisdom, and truth.

I now call in the highest, best, most loving possible guides and angels of the light, who can most serve. Please come in, connect, and channel through me now.

INTRODUCTION

W e, the guides and angels of the light, are here. We are a group of angels, spirit guides, and high vibrational light beings that have consciously joined together, merging our energy into one.

Individually, we each have a similar intent to assist humanity in the final push, the final step or nanosecond, if you will, to open to light. Our ultimate identity is one—one with all of creation, one with the cosmic mind, one with Creative Source, and one with you.

Many of the beings who now combine in this energy of one have individual personalities and traits. Some you know ... Jesus, Archangel Michael, Metatron, Orion, and Saint Germaine. Others behind the scenes quietly serve. Many come together from realms above to join light and increase focus and power. For indeed, there is more power accessed together, combined with focused intent, and this is closely aligned with the ultimate truth that we are one.

We are here, merging our energy as one to assist you now amidst great changes occurring on your planet. It is clear to us and many of you that your world is, indeed, in the midst of transformation, as the old comes up to be released in order to make way for the new. This same thing is happening in the lives of individuals, as collectively to the planet and throughout the entire universe.

You live in a time of change, evolution, and ascension. You may feel at times as though your life is crumbling around you, as change flows in from every angle. Indeed, it is a natural response for humanity to respond to change and the unknown with fear. Therefore, we come to connect with you now to say, "Do not be afraid but, rather, know that you too are connected to the divine plan."

At this time relax, and breathe, as you read. Find your center, breathe, and focus within, entering into a blissful, peaceful state. This state within cannot be explained, but it can be felt and experienced.

Feel your heart open. Feel yourself enter into your inner state of being, your inner realm in the area of your heart. Open and relax into this present moment and into the powerful energy of light, of divinity that does indeed exist in you. Open your heart to feel your vibration rise.

There is much talk in your realm these days about technology, and many of you would consider yourselves technologically advanced. But there is always room for growth. So we wish to draw your attention to the miraculous technology of your body, which science and your species is barely beginning to understand.

The technology of your heart when opened, when centered, allows you to connect beyond the physical realm, to connect with your light in the realm of spirit. Indeed, you are aware that you are a physical being, yes. Yet you are also spirit and source. When you use the advanced technology of your heart to open, to feel, to commune with the Divine, you make the great power of your open heart available to you always.

The transformation on your planet is not meant for you to struggle through with no reward at the end. Rather, you are consistently presented with opportunities to rise above all your limitations and to receive rewards beyond measure.

With your heart open, the power of love becomes fully accessible to you. In this now, with your mind calm, your energy expanding and merging with the Divine, you are refreshed and lifted, as you allow yourself to simply be.

Be present now and release any worries or feelings of struggle about the many changes in your life, or things in your reality that are crumbling, shifting, and evolving. The natural tendency is for you to want to know why certain things are happening and how they will work out.

But we say to you, there is great power in your simply surrendering to the power of love, and the power of the Divine. When you surrender, open your heart and say, I surrender, I trust in the process of life. I flow with the creative love of the universe. Then dear one, your unlimited power is accessible to you.

This shift occurring on your earth echoes throughout the entire universe and is divinely guided. You may feel as though you are being tested and challenged and that this is a time of great struggle. Remember, there is a higher purpose unfolding.

Take a moment to imagine the moon. And now imagine that you are standing on the moon, gazing down to Earth. Off in the distance, you can see this blue planet, the beautiful home on which you live. Imagine that you are looking down at Earth from beyond. And as if you have a high-powered camera, begin to zoom in on Earth.

Now specifically, zoom in on your life, viewing it from a completely new and outside perspective. Zoom in and notice how you relate to the world around you.

Do you trust in the process of life, flowing through your life's lessons, mastering love in the now? Or are you still buying into the illusion, the struggle, and the fear that has plagued humanity for so long? However you perceive yourself, it is likely that you are able to see areas for improvement, for growth, and ways in which you can be more fully connected to love in your life, to peace, balance, and joy.

This is the ultimate calling for you in your life. This is the purpose of the great transformation, acceleration of energy, and the ascension you and your planet are undergoing.

The old paradigm of manipulation, fear, and doubt, which has limited you and your species, no longer serves you in your growth. You are entering into a new era and a new becoming, leaving behind dualistic means of relating to the world—good and bad, right and wrong, light and dark. Your ego mind has served you in learning these lessons of duality. But we say to you now, you are moving beyond this.

When leaving anything behind, there can be resistance and struggle. Leaving behind fear, doubt, and duality may cause a sort of panic, as you naturally want to cling to what you know. And yet, a great flow of energy from cosmic consciousness, from the center of your galaxy and the central sun is entering in now to support this shift.

You as a species, and you as an individual being, are returning to the full knowledge of your power within, your connection to everything, and your ability to influence the world around you with your thought, your heart, and your inner intentions. In this way, your inner world shapes the outer physical world around you.

As we have said, there is a flow of conscious energy on earth—a wave, some may say. Your lesson is learning to ride this wave, for as you do, you can ride above the fear, doubt, and destruction. You can stay in love, and this allows you to integrate the new conscious energy on earth, and allows you to move towards your true purpose, your full light, and your true intentions.

Do not overthink these things, but rather, understand that you are here on earth to evolve, to continually grow towards fully integrating your spiritual self into physical form. You are here to remember your inner power and to create blessings and beauty in your world. This is the energetic flow and the opportunity available to you now by riding the wave of light, by opening your heart, by trusting in the universe, and by staying connected to love.

And of course, when you find you are being submerged—when you find you are not riding on top of the flow of life force energy but are being drowned in it, giving in to fear, to worry, to the illusion of suffering and pain—observe and take note. Notice what brought you to this state, what area of your life does not serve you in staying in love, in the higher realms, and in peace. This area of life, while it may bring you money, physical worldly pleasures or benefits, if it negatively influences your ability to stay in love, it is time for you to release it.

The time for struggle has passed, dear one. You, in your now, can ride the wave of light, can stay connected to your heart, to synchronicity and to love, bringing into your experience joy, authentic connection with others, and radical positive change. You hold the key for bringing your world and your life back into balance.

Powers that be will continue to try to hold on to the old paradigm to scare you and convince you that you are not safe, that the world is not safe, that reality is crumbling around you, and you should fear, worry, and give in to negativity, for there is no other solution. We say now, of course, there is another solution.

Indeed, this shift is all about returning you to power, to your light and your ability to authentically love yourself and all. Seeing through the illusions of the world and recognizing the truth that all is divine and you are living in the midst of a great shift, there is incredible support available to you within your heart, within the inner realms of light, truth, and love.

Release struggle, doubt, and fear, and tune in to your internal guidance system of knowing. Your emotions, point you in the right direction. Follow your heart, return to joy, and know that although, yes, you may be challenged now or in the future, much is changing and shifting. But all is divine and you are moving in the direction of realigning with your authentic truth. Let this motivate you to keep going and stay focused on opening your heart, on seeing through the illusion, and on living the life of love you are meant to, which you chose to be here on earth to experience radical, powerful, sustaining love.

We invite you now to imagine a pyramid of light all around you. Imagine this light beginning to fill your body with vibration, well-being, and love. Take a deep breath in to allow this into your experience. Now breathe out and let go, surrender, release doubt, fear, and negativity.

Enter fully into this now and know that a powerful energy indeed exists. New frequencies of light are present on the planet to help you on your path.

Open your heart, breathe, be and allow these energies into your experience. Allow love to guide you towards increased hope, peace, well-being, physical vitality, compassion, and authentic connection. This is what you are moving towards: balance with your earth and with all beings.

The increased energy at this time also amplifies your power of creation. So you have a choice, and truly, what you're focused on now begins to manifest in your experience. Allow your ideals to manifest by focusing on your authentic desires.

What do you want? Focus on the joy, the connection, the love, and your blessings, desires, and intentions will be created in the physical realm, beginning with your internal shift, as you surrender your mind and open your heart, trusting and flowing with the universe.

Let joy guide you, let love be your shining light, and let yourself go with the flow, riding on top of this wave of energy; not being carried under the current and not dragged into negativity, doubt, or fear. When these densities come up, release them. Imagine you are riding a golden surfboard of light and cruising effortlessly through the changes, flowing with the light wave on earth.

Now you are powerful to create change in your life and on a global scale. Open your heart and radiate love to bring about the highest, most loving, most beneficial possible situations and manifestations. Release struggle, release your fears, trust that a greater plan is in effect, and flow with this truth, this light.

Open your heart and keep it open to integrate the new frequencies present on your planet. Great changes in your world will come to be, so long as you trust and remain connected to love, to your open heart, and to hope. This is your purpose: to release the old and to rise into your power as a conscious creator, a human being filled with light and connected to authentic spirit, to source. You have all you need inside you.

Open your heart and connect with this light. Integrate your spiritual light into physical reality to allow the blessings, the love, the happiness, and the peace you so desire to be your primary experience. The energies of change support you in this now, but you must choose to accept, to be in love. And indeed, through this choice, anything is possible for you.

Open your heart, feel the light and the love all around you. Feel your connection to the universe, to your angels. Stay in this light, ride the wave of accelerated energy to manifest blessings, positive change, and hope for your future.

YOUR TRUE
SPIRITUAL SELF

There is much attention on your world now, in its current transitional period. What happens here indeed ripples out across time, affecting alternative realities of existence. There are, of course, beings who desire to remain in control of Earth. However, groups and guides such as ours are coming together in love to assist humanity in any way we can. We are here to help you become aware of your true power and not to fear it but to embrace it, radiate it, and use it to usher in peace, happiness, and well-being in your life and for your planet.

We are here to support you. You are now ready to know the connection to your true spiritual self, your spiritual body, your light, your power and oneness with divine source. And we feel that your fully connecting with this will empower you to make the choices that will indeed bring love once more to this planet in its truest form.

We are here to serve you now according to divine will and order, as you personally and collectively experience a time of great change. We greet you with frequency and divine light to assist you in connecting to the cosmic ray of crystalline energy present on your planet now.

We connect to assist you in elevating your vibration and more fully activating the light growing and building within you. Feel the light of the Divine broadcast all around you, in you, through you, and now relax as your vibration raises and your awareness becomes active and alert.

You are supported now in tuning in to the presence of the authentic you, your higher self, and your innate oneness with the Divine. Feel in your solar plexus and in your heart, your light growing and building within. Feel your power as a conscious being on planet Earth being restored.

We say to you now that you are the creator of your reality. Now is the time … you are ready to perceive your reality from this vantage point and to enjoy living the life of your creation. You are not separate from the Divine.

You are supported now in releasing your fears or feelings of victimhood due to the circumstances and events of your life, and in accepting that every event in life offers you opportunity for growth, for experience, to more fully connect with who you really are.

Who are you in the new energy? You are in complete oneness with Creative Source. This is the full awareness of who are you becoming.

Our hope is that you and all of humanity are returning to a place of peace and equilibrium, balance between the mind, body, and spirit. Remember and realize your connection to everything within the vast web of life on Earth, expanding outward into the cosmic universe.

In this now moment, you exist in a physical body in physical reality. But know that simultaneously occurring are parallel versions of reality in which you are playing out various scenarios in different physical and spiritual forms. From within this present moment and vantage point, you are able to tune in and be aware of yourself across the lines of time.

Through your ever-increasing awareness of the truth of who you really are, you are able to shine light and heal yourself. You are able to heal past, parallel, and future versions of yourself through the increased light and the growth you experience now.

You exist as a physical being here and now because this is the level on which you are able to become more aware. You are able to begin perceiving your reality beyond the third dimension, experiencing the richness, vitality and complexity of the energetic and spiritual realms.

And simultaneously to being physical, you exist in spirit, in a high vibrational state, in light, in joy, and in love. Through a calm mind and by opening your heart, you are able to fully tune in to this magnificent being that you are already in spirit. You are able to integrate your spiritual light into your physical reality on the earth. When you allow this integration, you truly are unlimited in your ability to create positive change in your world.

You may often think or worry about the state of affairs on your planet. But know that without the contrast, without institutions in your world crumbling, your consciousness would not be pushed to expand.

From our perspective, there is a wave of frequency and light energy broadcast from the center of the galaxy that Earth is now passing through. While you are collectively in this window, by simply opening and embracing the spiritual energy around you, you are able to become more aware of your truth as divine spirit manifest in physical form.

As a part of your increased awareness, this is all heading towards your being an accountable spiritual being on Earth. You are moving into living in harmony not only with your neighbors but with all creatures, physical and nonphysical beings on the planet—the trees, plants, and animals, which are all connected to you and are all made of the same creative source light as you. In truth, you are one.

From where you are now, if you are wondering what you can do and how you can help shift the trajectory of your species, we say to you that you are on this path. Continue to look within yourself to seek your ultimate truth.

We are here to help support you in this process. Right now, take a moment to relax, and tune in to your inner world, your inner state of being.

Accessed from within, incredible love is broadcast and available to you now. This light supports you in opening to send and receive more love. Through this, as a result, you will naturally further develop your unique spiritual gifts, skills, psychic abilities to be happy, aware, and observant in the now.

THE POWER
OF BELIEF

I ndeed, we are here. We are guides and angels of the light, and we greet you in this now moment. We are here to serve you according to divine will and order.

We are a group of angels, guides, and vibrational light beings that have consciously joined together, merging our energy into one. We are here to serve and assist you now, as you personally and collectively experience a time of great change.

Relax and breathe, and allow your energy to begin to lift. Quieting your mind and opening your heart will help you to more fully experience all that is conveyed now; for we speak to you in words, but we also broadcast energy and frequency.

This is a huge part of what you are learning, for you are more than physical. And when you tune in to your perceptions, impressions, and feelings beyond the physical reality, you open yourself up to experience the great truth of the multidimensional now.

CREATE YOUR REALITY ON AUTOPILOT

There is much talk in your world about thoughts and their ability to create your reality. We say to you, "Yes, you are the creators of your reality. But know that your thoughts are influenced by your beliefs and your emotions." Learning how to control your thoughts will have significant effect and impact on what you are able to manifest in your world. But understand that you do create on what we call autopilot.

When you're not consciously focused in on what you want, you're still creating. And so, learning to align your creation abilities on autopilot with your authentic self, your higher self, and your divine path will enable you to still be actively moving towards your goals, even when you are consciously engaged in some other expression or activity.

This is possible because your thoughts are secondary in creation, and the primary element that creates your reality is your belief. How you believe your world to be created draws that exact experience powerfully and magnetically to you. So those of you who believe the world is a cruel and hard place have no doubt attracted that cruel and hard experience to you.

But where do your beliefs come from? In reality, you are a multidimensional being. And although you are in physical reality now in a physical body, your spiritual self, your higher self still fully exists in connection to source and divine love.

For you see, you wanted to experience the physical world, planet Earth in the time paradigm you are in now, during a time in which your earth, humanity, and all of the inhabitants are undergoing an evolution, indeed, a transformation. And you wanted to be a part of it.

What is happening now is energetically tied to beliefs that date back to your ancient ancestors, back in time to when Earth was first created. Many beliefs are habitually ingrained in humanity through your mainstream media, religion, society, parents, and families that allow reality to be created on autopilot. This process is not flawed. However, deep-rooted fears, doubts, and beliefs of your inherent failure and your unworthiness no longer serve you. You, of course, are not the only being affected by this.

But as we said, all of humanity is undergoing an ascension process, astrologically and cosmically supported through the way in which Earth is now passing through a great band, a great flow of cosmic energy from the center of your galaxy.

CLAIM YOUR POWER

You can tune in to the elevated levels of light and consciousness to empower your creation now. Allow yourself to breathe. Relax and let your mind become clear and still. And through your open heart, tune in.

Tune in to your heart and feel your vibration raise, as you focus your intent on connecting with this energy, with this evolutionary beam of cosmic light. Open and breathe in the light, feeling it align with your physical body, feeling it lift your vibration.

You've been experiencing the effects of this energy for some time now. And understand that the tremendous light pouring in, in effect, shakes up, loosens up, brings to the surface those fears, doubts, and insecurities, which are ready to, once and for all, be released into the light and replaced with crystalline light of unconditional love.

As a human being, you have an unlimited opportunity now to clear out past conditioning, doubts, and fears, to release them into the light, and to redefine how you believe the world to operate.

When you question how you perceive your reality, when you challenge and question all your beliefs, you claim your power. For understand, so much of what you have been taught and what you believe is a limited view, a limited version of this world. The physical world is connected through a web of active energy to all of creation, to every now moment across time and space.

You in this now, by opening your heart, can choose to feel and vibrate in oneness with the energy that is divine love. Feel this love radiating through you, so that your body takes on a luminescent glow, and light fills your being, elevating your experience, aligning you with joy, love, and peace. As you consciously do this now, you enable yourself to stay in love.

In every now moment, it is essential that you release those beliefs, which no longer serve you. Often, these beliefs are so deeply ingrained that you believe them without question. We will go a step further to say that your beliefs are those areas of your reality which you accept unconditionally. Gravity is one such belief.

The way your world operates from your perception can be changed. We do not joke with you when we say that you are unlimited. But you must identify the beliefs that limit you, for this unlimited nature to truly enter into your reality.

CHANGE YOUR PERCEPTION OF YOUR WORLD

And so, this day we invite you to participate in an activity by simply observing yourself in your interactions with your world. Observe how you respond to the events of your life.

The objective is to write a list of things you believe about reality. Then go through this list of beliefs, your core beliefs about your world, and honestly ask yourself, Does this belief serve me and my highest path? Does this belief align with the reality I want to create?

And if the answer is no, you may find that you are still being affected by beliefs such as, "You are not smart enough." "You are shy." "You are not good enough to truly have what you want."

Release those beliefs with your conscious intention and begin to reprogram your subconscious mind using the power of words, affirmations in the "I am" form. I am the creator of my reality. I am living in a world that is filled with peace, bliss and harmony. I am living closely connected to the earth in balance and in love.

Go through all the beliefs you have identified and ask

yourself, Is there a more powerful, more positive belief I could replace this with? Through this process, you will begin to change how you perceive your world. And your perception of your world, beloved one, determines your experience. And so, your beliefs create your reality around you, and your perceptions allow you to experience this world.

In fact, you can expand your perceptions as well. When you are outdoors in nature, you are able to experience the physical beauty, balance, and divinity of the planet on which you live. But in this space, understand that you are able to become more aware to open your perceptions on many levels and to tune in to the natural world on a psychic, spiritual level energetically.

Share the vibration of love with the water, trees, plants, animals, and the earth on which you live, and you will find the love you send out returns back to you multiplied. So when you clean up trash from an area of nature, or when you meditate next to a tree while energetically loving and appreciating this being, you do send a ripple of your empowered, new perspective of the world across the lines of time.

As we have said, the growth you experience, and this expanded awareness that you open to experience in your now does not stay here. But indeed, it ripples out, bringing more joy and light into your many multidimensional selves, into the lives of your ancestors, and humans who have walked before you. This is energy healing across the lines of time.

CHALLENGE YOUR BELIEFS

Opening your energetic centers and tuning in, communing with the higher vibrations of love, peace, and joy present on your earth, greatly assists you in allowing these to be the foundational beliefs of your subconscious mind. And even when you're not consciously tuned in to what you want, to what you are creating, abundance, joy, and love are still manifesting when they're at your very core.

So challenge every belief that comes up in your life. Where does this belief originate? Was it psychically transferred to you prior to your birth from your parents? Is it something that has been ingrained in your bloodline for millennia, or is it a belief that you have created based on your experience in the world so far?

Whatever the case, allow yourself to feel the belief and release it into the light, replacing it with a belief that does serve you. When you are truly able to redefine what you believe about your world and bring these beliefs into alignment with positivity, love, joy, and abundance, then you are in the place we speak of, an unlimited being.

You are open and ready to allow the energy of your higher self to merge with your physical body, with your physical life, aligning you with great blessings, creating positive change in your world. Indeed, you become a way-shower for humanity, ushering out the paradigm of fear, doubt, struggle, manipulation, and control, and ushering in a new paradigm and a world of love.

You see, this is our ultimate objective for connecting with you: to help you live, embrace, and radiate the incredible love that is present on your earth. We know this will bring you joy, health, and happiness, and you are not far from this reality now.

Your focus, your openness, and your commitment to challenge the institutions that have helped you to form beliefs will empower your growth and healing. And so, be aware, question, and challenge your every experience and ask, What do I believe that has caused this to be, and what higher belief is ready to now enter my life?

TAP INTO YOUR UNLIMITED POWER

Humanity, and indeed the entire universe in which you live, is in the process of experiencing great change. And you, beloved one, are at the forefront of this change. That is why you are here, connecting with us in this now.

Remember, as you read these words and enable yourself to open your heart, you empower yourself to experience far more than can be expressed through words. We communicate with you through this written manner now, but we also communicate energetically across the multiple dimensions within which you exist. We connect with you now on an energetic and spiritual level alongside these words.

By opening your heart, you can feel and experience this love around you. This is very much the same process you are experiencing in your awakening. The change we speak of that is happening for your world is the acceleration of energy.

Understand that in the higher realms, energy moves at a

much faster rate, a rate you would call accelerated. For you then to experience the incredible love, peace, and joy that always exist in the nonphysical spiritual realms, there is a process of your energy lifting or accelerating, so you are able to fully tune in to and experience these subtle accelerated energies of the higher realms.

The benefit in this, of course, is that you are able to align with your unlimited power as spirit and as a spiritual being. When you came to earth, you knew this time period in which you were being born would be filled with many challenges and difficulties. But you also knew the incredible opportunity that existed and was available, and you eagerly signed up for an incarnation on earth.

Now that you are here, detached from the memory of the plan for your life, there can be confusion and turbulence. For these emotions are very much present in your realm—a realm that has been controlled for some time by forces of power whose intentions were not in line with the highest good.

But now where you stand, you are very much at a new beginning and an awakening of what we would call accelerating your energy to be aware of spirit in the physical. Yes, but still, you are also gaining awareness in the higher realms.

Your ultimate awakening will be in your ability to stand firmly in physical reality, grounded, centered, and yet, also experiencing fully the incredible love, joy, and light of the higher realms. Further, you are able to experience the full nature of your soul across the lines of time, in this reality, and in all other multidimensional expressions of you.

From this now moment, it is all possible. However, there are layers of illusion for you to work through to fully regain and integrate your power. Of course, this is why we are here to assist you in the process of removing layers of outdated beliefs, releasing layers of fear, manipulation and control, so that you, as an individual, can fully, proudly, and boldly step into your power.

And as you do this, as a human being, a divine spiritual being, you lead the way in consciousness for the rest of humanity to follow, to open, and to experience the great love that is possible for you in your time and in your work on earth. Many call this a balancing process, and it is true that balancing is required in your life to bring you back into alignment with what you ultimately desire. Balancing action with action, focused attention with meditative calm, and time to simply be.

You, as a physical being, are much more powerful than you have ever known. Your body has much more ability than you are aware of. Integrating your physical body with the light and spirit of your higher self is the quickest route to accelerating your vibration, so you are able to understand, experience, and tune in to the realms of the nonphysical, to your multidimensional nature.

And indeed, you are headed towards the experience of seeing, hearing, and knowing your full connection with your guides, your angels, and your higher self. Know that when you fully reach and enter this place, many of the problems on your earth—such as violence, hatred, and abuse towards the planet Earth from which you were created—will cease to exist.

Allowing more and more light into your being is, ultimately, your path towards fulfillment in this life. But as we said, there are many layers to your awakening. And yet, although each of your awakening paths and processes are unique in their own right, the underlying concept is that you are not in this alone.

Indeed, cosmic waves of energy from Creative Source and the center of the galaxy are flowing into your world now. And whether you are aware of these cosmic energies or not, you are being impacted by them, as they awaken you to those areas in which you are out of alignment with your true desires.

The strong energy pouring to earth will also bring to the surface the beliefs, the limitations, the blockages you have accepted as a part of your being. Those that no longer serve you must be released, and the energy assists you in this with a constant stream of cosmic light.

Begin to tune in to this now, allowing light to fill your body. Notice that, as you open your heart to this experience, you are able to feel good, to feel lightened in this energy. Return to the space of serenity, peace, and balance with your open heart by connecting to the realms of spirit and love. Regularly doing this will lessen and even eliminate much struggle and challenge on your path.

As we mentioned, challenges come up for you in this energy to draw your attention to areas where change is needed and to areas of your life that no longer serve you and your acceleration path. When you are tuned in and observant with a calm mind, you are able to know what changes are needed. You will know which emotion is yours and which emotions are others. You will know what is your truth and which emotion is lingering and bubbling up to the surface now for you to ultimately release.

When you find yourself feeling emotions of anger or sadness, anything that is on the scale of discomfort or negativity, remember that this is indeed tied to a thought or a belief. And so, allow yourself to feel whatever vibration is coming up and then release it.

Imagine yourself surrounded with the light. And with your words and your intentions, you are able to simply ask for that emotion or belief to be released and replaced with unconditional love, compassion, and joy. Then continue to go about your day grounded in love and peace, knowing this is your true authentic nature as a spiritual being, which you are moving into. You are here on earth to return to living in love, happiness, and well-being.

For you to fully align with this, your unlimited power in the light, there is a process that we will refer to as awakening. You will accelerate your energy, opening yourself up to more light, expanding your awareness, while questioning and challenging all of your core beliefs. These core beliefs are the ideas you accept about reality without question, and it serves you to challenge these now.

We suggest the process of writing down what you believe, noting those beliefs that limit you, and replacing them. This is the easiest route to massive growth and acceleration. Without this process, if you choose to ignore it, your growth opportunity does not stop there. However, the level of effortlessness, indeed, is altered. Without your conscious willingness to grow and change, the energies present now will trigger events or challenges on your path to show you a blockage or a belief that still limits you.

This is why so many newly awakened humans are creating great challenges, even tragedies, pain, illness, and suffering in life. Not because your world is inherently cruel, but because you have learned that through challenge and pain, you are able to grow, learn your lesson, and move on to the next. For this reason, it serves you to be extremely aware of how you feel. Your feelings, indeed, show you your point of attraction and where you are in the now.

And so, when you are feeling loved and light, when you are enabling the light energies of the universe to flow through you, and when you share this love with others, you feel good and happy. This is your validation that you are on track, moving in the direction of your highest good.

Yet in an instant, this can switch. And suddenly, you find yourself snapping, angry at something small in your reality, or saddened tremendously by a seemingly insignificant event. When these strong emotions come up, know that they are tied to more than the present moment, and they are coming up to draw this to your attention.

This is where your awareness comes into play, tuning in to your body not with your five physical senses of touch, taste, sight, hearing, and smell. These senses serve you, but you are able to perceive reality with nonphysical senses as well. Your imagination is a powerful tool for you to see beyond the physical. Your gut feeling and subtle ability to sense energy can alert your awareness when a choice you are about to make is not in line with your divine blueprint.

And so, you manifest strong emotions in your now to show you that, yes, these are still in you. And until you are able to fully release, there will be a cap, a limit to how high you can lift, to how much you can experience beyond the realm of the physical. So observe, if you can, what caused the challenging emotions to come up. What was the trigger, the catalyst for promoting change?

Be aware and identify where this emotion is coming from. Did someone push your buttons? Were you tuning in to a challenging experience or simply a past or parallel life experience? Know this is very possible, for as we said, you are multidimensional. And as you become more sensitive, you will be aware of painful emotions that limit you and are only tied to your current expression through your multidimensional nature.

Whatever emotion comes up that does not feel good, you can simply feel it, identify what it is, and then let it go, releasing it into the light. After you released this with your intention, imagine light all around and filling you, completely replacing the anger or pain with love. And then through this, you can rise again, connecting to more light, once again on your path of acceleration, moving towards your goal of full connection with spirit, light, and your higher self.

The world in which you live is a magnificent creation with everything existing in balance, fully connected. You can see this in nature easily. As one species, such as a giraffe, gains nourishment and vital energy through eating buds off a tree that graciously gives oxygen and food to the species, this is not a one-way exchange. For as the giraffe partakes from this tree, it enables the tree to reproduce, which it would not have done had the bud remained.

As you can see in this simple example, these two life forms are connected. But understand it is much more intricate and ever expanding than this. There are infinite connections, and in your now, you are connected energetically to all of humanity, to earth, and to all creatures.

And this is important, for it means when you, in your now, take the time to observe and tune in to your physical body, you may notice pain is stored in an area. Or a belief is stored at cellular level, perhaps one that suggests you are not good enough, or you are inherently bad.

This pain, this belief is connected to all humanity. When you empower yourself to release it, you truly lighten the energetic load of all humans you are connected to. When you take time to tune in to your heart, to meditate, to vibrate positively, to vibrate love, this ripples out across humanity, the web of life, and the lines of time, healing all humans and all multidimensional versions of you.

The power is in the now, ever more increasing your awareness, observing your role in reality, and opening to more love. As you open to this love, learning to let it flow through you and to respond to all of the challenges you encounter in life with love, your trajectory of growth will be a steady acceleration. Love is the power by which you manifest and connect with others. Love is what empowers you to fully connect with your authentic self, your spirit, your higher self.

So now, take a moment to simply affirm and repeat I love you, speaking to yourself, to your soul, to the core of your being. And in doing this, you will find you not only feel good, feel better, but you feel lighter. And in time, this love will indeed empower you to create radical, effective positive changes in your life and in your world.

You are here on earth to enjoy the physical reality; yes, to live in happiness and love, to experience life and all it has to offer. This does not mean to experience a limited version of your life based on the circumstances you have been born into. An unlimited experience is available to you now, but healing, growth and acceleration is needed for you to fully awaken to this empowered state as conscious manifestor, spiritual being of light, grounded in physical reality, creating and constructing positive change in the world.

You are here on earth to experience happiness, but much more than this, to transcend all limiting beliefs of which you have been conditioned. The beliefs of your family, your ancestors, and your society, do limit you to the extent you let them.

The first step is to become acutely aware of everything you believe. We cannot do this for you, but you can empower yourself to know all your beliefs by becoming an active observer of reality—observing how you respond to different people and situations, your instinct reactions, and how you feel when your beliefs are questioned, challenging everything in your world.

You do live in a world of illusion. And you see, much of this illusion that is limiting and has been in place, was created on earth by beings that did not have your highest intention in mind. They wanted the control and the power.

But you see, all beings on earth are able to open to power and love, to live in harmony and bliss, creating well-being and love on your planet. You are unlimited in this regard when you observe what you believe, when you release those beliefs that limit you, and fully step into your power as the creator of your reality.

You have control with your beliefs, your thoughts, and your emotions to manifest, to create your outer world around you, not through pain or struggle but through inner peace. Your outer world, too, will begin to shift and lift into alignment, into love and full connection with the spiritual realm when you make these inner shifts.

Indeed, you are here on earth to transcend all limiting beliefs from your ancestors, your family, yourself, and your society, releasing all limitations, and embracing positivity, well-being, harmony, and love. When these are the emotions behind your core beliefs, that fill you, then manifesting what you desire in the physical—peace, love, abundance, and happiness—your process becomes effortless.

There have been times in the history of the earth, in which beings lived in this high vibrational state we speak of, and manifestation was instant, empowered, and aligned with the higher vibrations of divine love.

And so, do you see the great power in releasing the beliefs that do not serve you, and empowering yourself with new beliefs of your creation that do?

Through this, you open to your unlimited nature, the nature of you as a spiritual being, an ascended master, a light being anchoring the light of the spiritual realm to earth, living life with ease, vibrant health and well-being, happiness and love. And you see, you are really not far away from this truth.

Sometimes it may seem overwhelming due to the vast amount of changes that are needed in your world, due to the crumbling of systems that have long been in power. But we say to you, "Hold on to love and hold on to the light. Allow these vibrations to flow through your being, to be at the core of what you believe." This will allow them to also be at the core of what you experience.

Your beliefs create your reality. The time of being a victim, of blaming others for your problems, for the challenges, for the difficulties in your world, for the areas you do not like, the role of victimhood is over. For in this new energy, in the light, you are infinitely powerful if you can bring yourself into alignment with believing this.

So do not feel overwhelmed at the large task in front of you. But rather, know there are a series of steps, a natural progression for awakening, accelerating, and ascending. You are in the middle of it now, and we are happy to help you align this transformation with positivity, for it can be.

Daily take the time to tune in to your heart and quiet your mind, imagining your mind is a white slate, clear, still and calm. Stare at the blank screen before you and then allow your conscious awareness to leave your mind and drop down into your heart.

Open your heart, feel the love and the energy of well-being. Open your heart to feel your connection with your higher self. Open your heart to grow and build the love therein, which is the source of your power. Open your heart to tune in to emotions that no longer serve you, which may be stored in this center. If you are experiencing anything other than love, release it, replace it with love, and open your heart once more. Practice this daily, for when you do, you are able to tune in to the realm of the nonphysical.

And again, you are ultimately in the process of bridging the gap, uniting the physical realm with the spiritual realm. It begins with you, but it will cover your entire planet, the entire cosmos.

There is a reunion of mind, body, and spirit. Your mind and body have been strongly connected. Now is the time to tie in the essence of your spiritual self, to bring your mind, body, and spirit into alignment with love. Allow love to shape your reality—beliefs of love to create your world, love for others, and love for yourself.

Practice this. Open your heart, radiate this light. This is your first step, radiating love.

YOUR
PERSONAL
POWER

As a human being living in a physical body in this now, you have an incredible amount of power. The ascension or acceleration process you are undergoing is essentially your realigning with this ultimate power and light within you.

Humanity as a whole has become disconnected from this power due to the misuse and manipulation of power by a few. But this power is your natural state of being, and the power you hold in your physical body is far greater than you, perhaps, can comprehend.

For although you have not fully aligned with this power in you, it is still there. And as you open yourself up, allowing the divine energies of love and life force to flow through you, this power is initiated; yet it is nothing new.

Indeed, you were conceived into this world through an active sexual power. And it was your own personal power that compelled you to leave the womb of your mother at the exact time of your birth to align with the astrological influences of your personality, which would most assist you in a specific lesson you came here to earth to learn.

And so, power is your natural birthright. It has been with you from before you even took your first breath and experienced your first moment in physical reality. But a widespread corruption in the physical taught you from an early age to bury your power, even to fear your innate power. In fact, there is a belief that absolute power corrupts absolutely.

But we see that you are able to open and integrate your power, using it to bring great blessings and progress to your physical realm. When power is used in alignment with love for the greatest good, it is used in alignment with your authentic purpose, which is love. Love and power combined truly have no limitations and serve and benefit all. The love we speak of is multifaceted and begins with self-love and forgiveness.

A widespread belief that has greatly influenced and controlled your society is the story of the fall of man from the garden of Eden, where Eve was tempted by the serpent with knowledge and curiosity to partake of the fruit from the tree of knowledge. And this act of curiosity, of wonder about the world around them, supposedly caused outrage in the eyes of God, who responded by casting out Adam and Eve from Paradise into the cruel and harsh nakedness of the physical realm.

So humanity was branded as sinners and, whether this is fully true or not, this vibration of sin is carried by humanity now. Original sin passed down through generations, and from the time you were birthed, has caused great corruption.

For as we have addressed, your thoughts and beliefs about your physical world greatly influence the reality you experience. This includes generational, collective, and subconscious beliefs.

And so in this now, it would behoove you greatly to take a firm stance in self-love, appreciation, and respect, forgiving yourself for any sins or transgressions you feel you may have committed in your life, and loving yourself fully in this now. Forgive your ancestors and forgive other humans sharing this realm. To forgive and love yourself completely, exactly as you are now (connected to everyone and everything), is the first step towards truly reawakening your power in the light.

Filling yourself up with love, positive thoughts, affirmations, and empowered beliefs can create a strong foundation for awakening. Self-love will then propel you effortlessly along the path of awakening. Therefore, it benefits you to regularly affirm I love and approve of myself.

Feel the vibration of great love for you and your uniqueness. Feel great love for who you are, for this love does not end here. For the love you feel for yourself, filling yourself with love, enables you to then overflow this love to others. And it is through giving and receiving love that you begin to evolve your personal power, empowering yourself to grow personally and spiritually in love.

Each time you catch yourself in the moment responding with fear or anger, stop and observe this reaction, and allow it to pass through you. Release these lower vibrations into the light, and return to love. When you are in a state of love, happiness, and well-being, this is your point of attraction.

And these underlying beliefs, thoughts, and perceptions, indeed, create the world around you.

So when you feel good, loved, and excited about the reality you are creating, you attract more of this goodness to you. Love attracts more love, compassion, and works by magnetizing peace and compassion to it. It is possible for you now to stay in love and peace always—not easy, but possible indeed.

The vision we hold of your world is exactly this: an illuminated realm of well-being, kindness, and love where the forces of fear, anger, and pain are no longer needed.

These lower vibrational energies you have been experiencing in your physical reality thus far have the purpose of awakening you and showing you where you are not in alignment with your highest path, through feelings of discomfort or tension. And so, when you feel these things, know they are not your ultimate experience. But rather, they are coming up simply to draw your awareness to shift and move from where you are now along the emotional vibrational scale towards love.

Yes, transitioning directly from fear to love can be challenging, and it is a big step. And so when you are in fear, do not judge yourself or run from the fear, but feel it, observe it, and then release it, and let yourself simply be.

From this state of being with a clear mind, a blank screen in front of your mind's eye, and an open heart, you can make the transition. You can fully enter into love, which in turn, activates the power for positive creation in you. You are the creator of your reality with your beliefs, your thoughts, and your emotions. And the universe you live in does not discriminate in regard to what you are creating.

So when you are in fear and anger, attracting more fear and anger to yourself and the universe, your angels respond, not judging what you choose to experience, but simply allowing your creative power to dictate how you feel about the world around you.

Worrying about the outcome of an event is likely to manifest the exact outcome that you worried would take place. This is why it is so important for you to be an active observer of yourself. When you are in the role of observer, you are experiencing an aspect of yourself other than your ego.

Ego is the main source of problems, fear, doubt, and negativity in your world, largely due to conditioning in the fight-or-flight response, which has been ingrained in the human ego from the time of your ancestors, who lived in caves and dealt with wild beasts. The ego served then to quickly assess a situation and know whether to fight or flee. But now today in reality, this automatic conditioning greatly limits your ability to create.

Love empowers you to take back control over this creation process. Observing yourself in the now, choosing to radiate well-being and love, aligns you with a powerful point of attraction. And so, when you are in the vibration of love, you send out a thought such as, I want a fulfilling relationship, or I want a job that brings me joy and abundance, or I want an opportunity to serve and connect with the earth in a loving and sustainable way.

When you send out an intention like these from a place

where you are feeling happy and loved, vibrating with the goodness, light, and love of the universe, you are aligned with your power. And so, your intention is supported with the power of love.

As long as you are able to stay in this love, as you move forward in your life, the intention you desire can effortlessly flow in, merging with you in the physical. The key here is love. The key is your positive vibration and feeling good, sending the message to the universe: This thing I desire, I love and feel good about, I want. Staying in the vibration of love means you are in a state of allowing so your manifestation can flow in.

A simple exercise for this begins with imagining your mind is a clear slate, a white screen, and then dropping your awareness down into your heart, your center and opening. Imagine light all around that pours in and fills you, and let this light attach to your aura, to your body.

Breathe it in and let your vibration raise, entering into this moment, being fully present in love, well-being, and joy, and activating your inner power and your inner light.

Then focus on what you want to create, a physical object, a person, an opportunity, increased clients, vibrant well-being. There's no limit as to what you can create when you are aligned with your power, for you are unlimited.

Right now, focus on what you want. Imagine it is somewhat far away from you, but that you, in this moment, are filled with light. Imagine a golden spiral of light flowing out from your heart into the universe, and now it is heading towards the object of your desire, of your creation, powered by the energy of love, well-being, and joy.

Vibrant golden light is pouring into you and then spiraling out of you, continuing to flow into you and then pouring out into the physical. Now this energy reaches the object of your desire, your manifestation and wraps all around it. Imagine golden light swirling all around what you desire, until your desire looks as though it's surrounded in an orb, a sphere of golden light.

The light spiral from your heart now reverses with your intention. As this object is now magnetically drawn to you, the reversed spiral pulls it in. Breathe and give gratitude for this thing you are creating. Feel good, feel loved, love yourself and feel that which you desire being drawn to you.

There should be a click, a point when you realize the object you have magnetically attracted is effectively with you. The essence of your creation is now being held in your heart.

Open your heart even more to feel more love for yourself now and for the future in what you are creating—love. And know that indeed this creation of your design has been drawn to you. It is now in the process of manifesting, of being created.

From here, your crystal clear intentions are of utmost importance. For thoughts of excitement about this manifestation drawing into your life bring it more quickly. But doubts and fears that it will not work for you actually push what you want further away.

The process of allowing this into your life now is essentially your choosing to trust that it is coming. You can do this by choosing to return to love in every now moment.

There will be challenges, obstacles, or emotions that come up which are contrary to what you want, contrary to love. These are very much tests for you in the now. It is your choice to return to love. Trust and allow your desired manifestation to flow in your life. Trust that it is in the process of creation.

And then as you stay present and in a state of love—in other words, staying in your power and in the light—this empowers you to know the right time to take action. If action is required, which it likely is, being in the now, in love, in your power, allows you to know if you are needed in a physical location or to take a specific action to bring what you want into alignment.

Being fully present in the moment, connected to the love, can even allow the object of your desire to manifest effortlessly in your reality, for you are connected to your power, your love, and your light in the now. Or there may be some action required. Either way, as you know, in this energy all things are possible.

As you begin this process, it is very important for you to be the active observer of yourself, and to note when you are in love and when you are not. And when you catch yourself vibrating with insecurity, fear, negativity, or density, remember that these emotions no longer serve you. They come up to be released, so they can easily flow through, up, out of you, and back into the light, to be replaced with love.

Just like that, you're able to return to your power, to the compelling point of attraction that is love. Through opening to your power, all things are possible. Let your creative imagination spark, play, and realize what it is you really want.

Through love and conscious intention, you are able to claim your power and begin to use it to manifest blessings in your life and in your world.

YOUR UNLIMITED CREATIVE POTENTIAL

T he present moment is ultimately where you are able to accelerate your growth, expand your awareness, and empower yourself to connect with your inner power and light. The now moment is where you can access your ability to create reality with your thoughts, perspectives, actions, and beliefs.

There is an acceleration of energy, which you are a part of on your planet. This acceleration is greatly influenced by the forces of your sun, the orb of warmth, light, and vitality that allows you to experience life on earth as you know it.

Through an energetic shift and acceleration of energy, your sun is playing a vital role in the transformation process, broadcasting light codes of consciousness into your world. Indeed, increased light and crystalline energies of activation are present now. However, it is up to you, the individual in the now, to choose to incorporate these energies of consciousness.

You are ultimately responsible for your growth and for the reality you create. Physical reality in which you live offers an opportunity to express your creativity through all of creation.

Your words hold great power and focus. With specific intent in writing, you actually can begin the process of manifestation. Your ancestors long believed writing to be a powerful and special form of magic with influence to create in the physical world. And indeed, every creation now present on your earth, the good and the bad, began with a thought, an intention.

And so, where you are now, a human awakening to your unlimited potential in the light, it serves you greatly to be the active observer of your reality. In your present moment, practice observing your thoughts, feelings, and beliefs. And from the outside perspective of the observer, you are able to see and experience firsthand that you are far more than a physical being.

You can take this a step further by calming your mind and opening your heart to tune in to the light energies of your higher self, present in the realm beyond the physical. You are able to go through the process of integrating your spiritual light into the physical realm, and understanding, embracing your power.

With a clear mind, focused on the intentions and desires you wish to create in your reality, you can create in the physical world all that you desire. You can accelerate yourself to the highest level of awareness in the present moment. You are here now and you have already begun awakening.

The accelerated energies on the planet serve to help you focus inward, to recognize the symbols and the patterns of your life. The patterns have brought you into this very moment, and you are able to consciously project where you are headed. All your past experiences, including the contrast points both bad and good, were in preparation for this now, where you are able to choose the future you will create.

Accelerated crystalline energies on your planet offer you support in this process of expanding and increasing your awareness. But without your conscious choice, this process does not take place. Indeed, you are an important part of this puzzle, for it is your choice to tune in to the new vibrations of accelerated light, and to incorporate new energies, ideas, and frequency into your life.

In the present moment, your power to create change in your reality exists. You are here to learn how to experience and manifest with energy, to use your uniqueness to create a new version of reality by your design. The authentic truth of who you are is an unlimited being in an illusion of limitedness, learning to remember your full power to create.

All of humanity has this creative power. Each of you, in your now, with your thoughts, feelings, and beliefs, cause your outer world to take form. The long-standing paradigm of fear and control on your earth realm is, of course, still an option for what you may create. However, by releasing the past conditioning and beliefs of your society, of the media, of those in control, you are able to claim the reality you desire—not one rooted in fear and destruction, but a reality of authentic connection and love.

In your now, you can begin to make this change. You do this by being peaceful, still, and calm, observing your reality, and responding to the challenges and changes of life with love. Love activates your cells. Love assists you in remaining in a state of allowing, ready to receive. And through this vibration of love for yourself, for others, for your planet, love brings your being into alignment, so you can integrate and choose the lighter frequencies now present on earth.

It serves you greatly to affirm and claim responsibility for yourself as the creator of your reality, and to empower yourself to release the limited versions of who you are and what you can be, to open to your inner light and strength, your power through love. And it's giving love and receiving love. Through this power of love and focused intention, positive changes in your world are made possible.

There are signs and circumstances that have caused you to doubt. And outside physical situations, corporations, and financial institutions may seem like some of the greatest challenges at this time. But understand from our perspective, we see this as further pushing you to awaken beyond the illusion you have created thus far—an illusion grounded in fear, control, and lack, an illusion that you are limited—when in reality your authentic truth is as an unlimited being.

The sun, the stars, the cosmos broadcast waves of energy to Earth with the purpose of awakening and empowering humanity, for you to fully open to your power as a creative being. And it is through actively observing yourself, your thoughts, responses, choices, and feelings that you ultimately determine the core belief patterns and limiting belief systems, which presently rule and create your reality.

When you observe this and pinpoint the beliefs that limit you, you are able to release them, replace them with positive thought, with the intention of where you desire to move, of what you desire to create. There is incredible power in this process. And as each unique being of light, each member of humanity goes through this awakening and accepts responsibility for creating life, then finally, as a collective species, you will be able to return to creating an existence of peace, love, and harmony as unlimited beings.

The ultimate goal of this awakening is to bring you back into alignment and connection with your higher unlimited self. It is true that part of experiencing reality in the now, in which you are, was becoming disconnected from the source of power, from your higher self, and from the knowledge of yourself as a multidimensional being. You chose this separation in order to more effectively learn how to manage energy, how to create in the physical world, and as a sort of experiment.

The time of being separated from higher self and experiencing the illusion of being limited has offered many learning opportunities. But in this now, you can realign with this powerful being who does know your ultimate specific path and purpose here on earth and the creations that will most fulfill and excite you.

Your higher self knows what is for your highest good and the highest good of the planet and all humanity. And so, when you accelerate your energy by choosing to lift in conscious love, when you break through the paradigm of limitedness and illusion, you claim this creative power as your own.

Your physical body contains great potential too. Nourish the body you are in with good purified water and natural foods. Vegetables and fruits and plants sustain your body in a state of balance, which allows you to function in vibrant health, and your mind is able to more effortlessly remain clear and calm.

Then you are in the position of power, ready and able to set the intentions of what you want, to put them into the magic form of writing, to reclaim your power to create the world around you, and to manifest many blessings in your life.

Increased awareness is your purpose now. As you actively observe and question reality in its current form, ask yourself why things are in the state they are, and what you can do to contribute to creating positive change. When you observe yourself in the now, pay attention to the symbolic nature of your thoughts. As you observe the cyclical patterns that have brought you to here, your higher self speaks to you in the language of symbols, sounds, shapes. And by learning to understand what this means, you can know the path of your higher self and highest good.

But even if you are not yet at this level, choose to be in the now, choose to love in the now. Choose to open your heart, open your mind, and experience your world with all your senses. And through your foundation of love, your focus, you are empowered to choose the new energies that accelerate you on your path.

Great growth is available now in a compressed time, and the accelerated energy of this sometimes-tumultuous process of transformation brings this gift. The breakthroughs you experience now, the new levels of light and the positive creations, affect all of existence. The blessings from remembering your unlimited power flow across the lines of time, bringing this enlightened, empowered energy to all past, parallel, and future realities and paradigms.

The love you feel in your now can be nurtured to grow, to open your innate psychic gifts and abilities, to focus your creative power, and to bring you into alignment with what you ultimately desire in this new energy.

The now moment is your opportunity to create change. And love is the fuel, the fire that makes it all possible. Ascension is the process of acceleration, the process of reuniting with your power, with your higher self, with the power of love. Choose love in your now to allow many blessings to manifest in your life.

Where you are sitting now, allow yourself to relax. Relax your jaw, your neck and your shoulders; relax your mind and your body. Tune in to your heart and visualize golden spirals of light all around you. You are imagining or, rather, tuning in to the crystalline energies of acceleration broadcast by your sun. Relax to allow these energies into your being.

Imagine the light swirling all around you. Breathe in deeply and, as you inhale, imagine that light is filling your body. As you exhale, release all tension, fear, and negativity. And as you inhale, you are filled with light, love, and vitality. As you exhale, this love that now fills you is sent out to your world.

Breathe in love and light. Breathe out love and light. Breathe in the light to accelerate your vibration, to connect with your truth, and to empower your intentions and your desires.

Have fun with this. You are a creative being. That is why you are here. You are learning to create with energy, thought, feeling, emotion, and action in the physical world.

Let love be your guide. Let joy be your compass. And with love and joy navigating the continuing changes and the world around you, you can transform into its highest level of experience and your highest level of awareness.

The growth available to you now is unlimited and unending. But you must choose to tune in, in the now, to allow these energies into your body and your life. Creative control is yours, should you choose to accept, should you choose to release the limitations, the illusions, the fears, and the doubts of your world.

By choosing love, integrating your power, and creating the blessings you deserve and desire in your life, you are unlimited with love and joy as your guide. Follow these, follow your heart and the divine path of goodness and positive change will begin to merge with you in your now, as you open more fully to the light and to your power.

COMMUNICATING WITH YOUR HIGHER SELF

Y ou now have the opportunity to fully ascend and fully awaken to the unlimited power of your higher self. You have the opportunity to fully empower yourself to claim your role as conscious creator of your reality, letting go of any feelings of victimhood.

When you experience something in your life you did not want to create, recognize it is your creation, nonetheless, and that it has been created for some learning and for growth.

You are an unlimited spiritual being in the physical realm, experiencing the illusion of being limited. You are here for growth. It is through your challenges you are often motivated to grow, to look deeper, to expand your perceptions and awaken to the remembrance of your true nature as an unlimited spiritual being.

Open your heart, quiet your mind, and tune in to your feelings, knowing, perceiving and imagining, at first, that divine light, guides and angels are all around you. The more you consciously try to perceive reality beyond your physical realm, the more quickly you will open to fully experience the energies that are present.

Your physical world is connected now through a vast and intricate web to all that is. You are in no way isolated from the spiritual realm, from the heavens, or from the cosmos. Rather, right now from where you are in your physical body, you are able to tune in to all these vibrational frequencies. And when you tune in to the vibrational frequency of the higher realms, your sun, light beings, stars, and angels, even you cannot help but raise your own vibration. And as we have mentioned, raising your vibration is the direct path for you to fully and authentically connect with your full power, your full being, your true self, as an illuminated spiritual being of light.

Of course, your every now moment is your opportunity to go within. And it is within you that you are able to gain the most knowledge, wisdom and understanding about your authentic truth and unlimited light; all you need is to access within.

Your heart chakra is an amazing energy portal which, when opened, allows you to fully tune in to your higher self, to the messages and guidance of your angels, and to clear knowing of your connection with the spirit and of your innate and powerful ability to manifest in your physical realm.

Manifestation and learning does not happen or come from outside you, but rather from within you. With your beliefs, your thoughts, and your emotions, you begin to create in the physical. From within the realm of the nonphysical, your physical world takes form.

All the knowledge you desire and seek can be learned in a roundabout way through reading and studies, through looking for truth outside of you. But until you get this truth and are able to tune in to your inner being through being still and calm in the moment with your heart open, you will be unable to access all the infinite wisdom of the universe. This information is light and it can be accessed within you.

And so, by opening your heart, quieting your mind, and tuning in to the light all around and within you, great advances can be made in your knowledge, in your physical vitality, in the joy, compassion, and love you experience. These are all lifted and empowered through light.

When you are wondering about a choice you want to make in reality, such as whether your ideas are truly in line with your highest and greatest path, go within to find the answer. You could spend hours and days researching the ins and outs of the decision you want to make, or you can simply check in with your heart.

Breathe and open your heart. Just sit, feel, breathe, imagine you are surrounded with light, and know that your guides and angels and your higher self are with you. Feel their energy, feel the divine love, light, and life force energy flowing through you.

Open your heart, and then ask your soul, your higher self, the universe about the decision you are wondering about. Ask about the idea you are playing with, a future potential manifestation. Ask Is what I am attempting, working on, and creating truly for my highest good?

And now, drop into your heart more and feel your answer. How do you feel? Are you feeling loved? Are you feeling even lighter? If so, this is a sign that your idea, your intention is in line with your highest path. Move towards it.

Or when you ask, does your energy drop? Do you feel weaker like you are being pulled away? Do you feel pain? This is an indication that your answer is no. This is a simple way of checking in and knowing your truth.

Trust your feelings, your intuitions, your gut, for they truly serve you well. And as you practice this, checking in with your soul and your spirit, the answers you receive will transition from a simple feeling to the clear, concise answer about what is in line with your highest good.

You can create anything you desire in this world by opening to the crystalline energies of light and love and using them to empower yourself to manifest in your world. This can be easily accomplished, or it can be a more challenging path. This depends on whether what you are moving towards is in line with the intention of your higher self, your heart, your soul, the divine blueprint for your life, and your true intentions about what you want.

If you are planning on manifesting something that goes against this intention, and you move forward, working on drawing it to your life, be assured there will be bumps, challenges, and struggle. The manifestation will not come easily, and this is not because you cannot have it, but you are challenged because your attention needs to be drawn to a higher possible manifestation. Your soul is helping you to realize that what you are going after is somehow short of what you truly want at soul level and what you can create.

When your manifestations are in line with your highest good and your divine path, they will flow easily into your life without struggle and challenge. And so, it does serve you greatly to quiet your mind, open your heart, and ask, Is what I am focusing on, is this thing truly in line with my highest good?

Now quiet your mind and imagine it is a blank white slate before you. Open your heart. What message does your higher self, your soul give you now? Is this the highest possible manifestation for you? Does it feel good? Is your higher self validating your question with feelings of love and light, ease and well-being? Or is there a challenge that's already coming to mind? Are you feeling weakened or drained?

You have an answer. Use your intuition, your gut feeling, and your imagination to let this appear. Know your higher self is communicating with you, is answering this question. Thank your higher self for this unlimited guidance and knowing it provided.

Know that this simple act of checking in with your spirit and your soul is so powerful because if you did feel a drop in your energy or perceive some challenge, obstacle or a negative feeling, you know the answer was no. Then focus on and pursue a higher manifestation. Tune in to the knowing of what this is, and remember that all the knowledge, wisdom and guidance is already accessible from within you.

Open your heart and ask, What will bring me the fulfillment, love, and happiness I desire? What manifestation is for my highest good? And let your mind be still. Tune in to your feelings, and let the subtle energies of your psychic impressions come in.

You have physical senses, but you also have intuitive and psychic senses through which your higher self will communicate. Open these receptors and allow the knowledge, the vision, the feeling of what truly is in line with your highest and greatest path, for the highest and greatest good of you and everyone in the earth, and what is the higher version of the manifestation you can create.

Let your higher self show you this, attune you to this, and let you feel this. For when you are in the process of creating, of manifesting that which is in line with your divine blueprint, your highest and best possible plan for your life, it will flow easily and effortlessly with assistance from your higher self, from the universe. When things are meant to be, they will be. They come easily and without struggle.

Remember this when you are struggling to create something you want. Experiencing struggle is a warning sign or a flag, and an indication that a shift is needed. The challenge shows you that you can perhaps rise above it and manifest something even greater than you were initially shooting for. And all you need to do is tune in, check in.

The more you practice, the more you open your heart, ask, and commune and connect with your higher self, your spirit, the clearer the guidance will become. It just takes practice. When you start, allow yourself to feel, and then let this feeling evolve into clear knowing and understanding. And use this magical ability to focus and create what you really want at soul level that brings you fulfillment.

As you practice connecting with your higher self to know your path, your connection is increased and strengthened each time you try. So daily practicing serves you to stay more on course. And also, you will consistently be moving towards holding even more of your light, as a spiritual being, accelerating your energy, expanding your awareness, allowing you to create and experience all the love, joy, abundance, peace, and fulfillment of your physical realm and the spiritual realm.

Remember that all you need is within: guidance, knowledge, courage, and strength. Practice awakening and opening your heart to fully allow your divine love, your higher self to merge with you. Claim your power. Create blessings in your life.

PERCEPTION IS REALITY

U nderstand that our goal to help you align with love and happiness is not simply for our well-being. Indeed, you gain a unique advantage in your ability to manifest the physical world to your liking.

When you are in the vibration, the emotion, the feelings of love, joy, and happiness, it is important for you to recognize that your love and happiness are your choice. Many of you feel that love and happiness is something outside of you, and these emotions will be felt and experienced when you align with the right job or the right partner, the right series of physical events. Then you will be able to stay happy and stay in love. And we say to you, it is the other way around.

When you are able to be happy and in love right now and in every now, regardless of your outside circumstances and the world around you, you are in a position of power. When you are happy and in love, your vibration is a positive place. And your point of attraction is focused towards bringing you more of what you innately want, more to make you happy, to bring love and well-being into your life.

If you are not currently happy with many things about

your reality, you may see this as a great challenge—being happy when you are simply not. Understand, however, that by working with these methods we have shared with you, by changing your beliefs about yourself and your reality, by practicing radical self-love, encouraging, honoring, and nurturing yourself, you can find love and happiness in your now, regardless of what is going on around you.

A healthy mind, heart, and body are yours for the taking, and these things more effortlessly flow into your life when you are happy and when you are vibrating with the emotion of love. It has been scientifically proven now that there is a tangible advantage when you are happy. Your business ventures will become more prosperous, and you will more easily attain the level you desire. Your health will remain more balanced, and you can claim the vital well-being that is your birthright. Your body is able to fight disease, maintain well-being, and flow with vitality, when love and happiness are the thoughts powering your being at a cellular level.

When your emotions drop, when your vibration drops, when your thoughts and beliefs spiral downward into blame, victimhood, doubt, and fear, your immune system is weakened. And so, being happy is the best immunity booster you can nurture.

Being in love is the best way for you to take your abundance to the next level, and for your finances to reach the state you truly desire. Love and happiness are the foundation for you to create anything you want in life. A partner, the right job, a business opportunity, well-being, vitality, and health are all strengthened and helped by feelings of love, happiness, and well-being.

There's not one time of day, one moment in your day, or one specific day of the year when you must be in love and be happy to draw to you what you want. But you see, in your process of gaining awareness and awakening, you are being asked, or rather, you are being empowered to choose love and happiness in your now. For in your now, in every now moment, you are actively creating, manifesting, and drawing to you, your future experiences in life. In this now, the thoughts and beliefs of every member of humanity mix and weave together in an intricate web of creativity by design to create your physical realm.

As you begin to shine, to project a more positive vision of tomorrow, releasing fear, focusing on and manifesting love, well-being and happiness in your life, the collective experience slowly begins to change. And this change accelerates as more individuals become empowered and step into their roles, claiming light, living in love, happiness, and joy, and through this, drawing to you more happiness and love.

It is not always easy to love in your realm or to be happy, we understand. But by taking the view that your challenges, hard experiences in life, and difficult people who push your buttons and test you in ways to alter your course even more, you have a default reaction of anger, judgment, or pain. This creates a great opportunity for growth. The default reaction comes from your core beliefs and the conditioning from the time you were born.

But this, of course, can be changed right now. In your now, observe. How do you perceive your world? Are you falling into the trap of victimhood, or are you able to confidently love your path and your life, radiating happiness in your now moment?

When you do this, you are at a positive point of attraction. In responding with love, you are drawing what you ultimately desire to you. Love is the state of allowing and the power by which all in the universe are connected. Become intimately familiar with love and happiness and choose to respond with them, even in situations in life where these are not your default reactions.

Replace anger with love. Replace frustration, which you normally feel, with feelings of acceptance, happiness, and understanding. And when you do, you release a great weight from your shoulders, and you are able to stay in a positive vibration.

Remember, when you are in a positive vibration, in your now moment, consciously allowing more and more of your higher self, divine love, and life force energy into your life, through feeling happy, well, and loved, you are accelerating your evolution and are drawing to you the things you want. And from our perspective, you are here on earth to transmute and transcend fear and negativity and to replace them with love, well-being, and happiness.

When all humans choose to let love, light, and peace be the foundation for creating reality, much of the complex turbulence and chaos in your world will cease to exist. This change does not happen overnight, but it happens one being at a time, one now moment at a time, and one conscious choice to express love in the midst of challenge, happiness in the midst of struggle, and to view life as a blessed and wonderful adventure you are lucky to be a part of.

Giving thanks in your reality brings more for you to give thanks for. Loving others attracts more for you to love. This is the path of least resistance and, as you flow around the river of love and happiness, you become positive change on autopilot in your world. Let love and happiness be your default reactions, the emotions you experience in your now.

Growth may be required from where you are now to fully align with living this way in the light. But do not worry. Remember, this is what you are overcoming. When you feel these things, allow yourself to feel them, and don't bury them. They will come up again if you do.

Feel whatever you are feeling, identify the source of this blockage, the belief behind it, and then release it into the light. When you have released the denser vibrations within you—the blockages, the challenges, and the struggles—nothing can hold you back from accelerating your vibration even more.

So once you release something that no longer serves you, clear your mind, open your heart, and lift. Allow light to flow into you, radiating light and well-being. And when you do, happiness, love, and the intentions and desires you are focused on can easily flow into your reality.

You are the creator of your reality. Through releasing thoughts of being a victim and thoughts that reality happens to you, you can change the course of your experience forever. Perceive reality in a happy, loving and fun way, and you will manifest more of this in your experience. Be happy, choose love. Even in the greatest of struggles, you can learn to let these be your responses. Every time you share happiness or love with another, you cannot help but attract more happiness or love back into your life.

The human web is intricately connected through the matrix of divine love. Accepting, choosing, and allowing love to be the predominant emotion and force you experience in life creates a fundamental shift in the web of reality. You no longer project limiting beliefs, fears, and doubts into the subconscious mind, into the collective consciousness. Instead, you create positive change.

With love and happiness, you help everyone else to make this change as well. You are all connected. And so, when you, beloved one, reach a new level of vibration, a new level of awareness, empowerment, and ability to radiate love in every now, you help others to awaken initially or to begin to shift the balance of fear and love in their life, allowing more well-being and more light.

There is an unlimited source of goodness in this world. It is an abundant universe. With your thoughts and beliefs, you create your reality and draw to you the experience of your design, the experience you truly desire. Get rid of any limiting thoughts, let love be your foundation, and let happiness rule your life. Then you will perceive reality in a fun and enjoyable way, and you will create a lasting and significant contribution in these changing times.

So much change is needed in the world. Violence, chaos, and turbulence are on their way out, as one conscious being at a time makes the choice to be empowered in the now moment, choosing love over violence, choosing happiness over fear, sadness, and doubt. This is your choice in this now and in every now. Choose wisely and choose happiness and love, and the rest of your path will flow into view.

You are unlimited with the power of light, love, and joy on your side. Let these things determine what you do and how you experience your world. You are a leader for an earth in crisis and in times of change. Be this leader by boldly and confidently stepping in and choosing love, being happy and compassionate.

With this, great change on a global scale will begin to take form. It already is. And as the majority of humanity reaches the ability to choose love in the now, your paradigm will be transformed.

We eagerly await this moment, living in this now until love becomes the predominant force of your realm, and it will. Trust and move in the direction of your goals, feeling emotions of love, happiness, and well-being for where you are, and believing what you want will come to be.

YOUR POWER TO CREATE POSITIVE CHANGE ON EARTH

You have a level of creative control in your reality. You are involved in a complex game, a complex story written according to divine design. You are here, present in the now, in the physical realm, and in a physical body, and you are far more powerful at this time than you are aware.

It is your beliefs that you allow to limit you, which limits your power. But the truth of your ability, the truth of the possibility now is anything.

With your thoughts, your beliefs, and your feelings, you create your outside world. The thoughts, beliefs, and feelings of all humanity merge to create your experience. And although there are, indeed, millions of humans contributing to this creation, your intentions, your ideas, your wishes and your desires are valid.

You, beloved one, through your awakening and your becoming more aware in the now moment, claim your power by choosing love and happiness and focusing your mind on what you do want. And so, you are able to create change on a grand scale in your world.

The earth and its inhabitants have been at the same crossroads before. Incredible potential is before you, incredible opportunity for growth. In the past, humanity has chosen fear and destruction, to end the game and begin again. But now, as you empower yourself in this new energy, as you vibrate with love, peace, and understanding, you send out the blueprint for an enlightened tomorrow.

With your love and happiness, you truly can bring about a great shift in the realm of earth through the process of opening to even more of your spiritual self and accelerating your energy to vibrate well-being and happiness always.

With this choice in the now, you can create greatness in your realm. You can impact all of creation by being positive, centered, and present in the now moment, by first observing how you respond, and how you perceive your world around you. And then take this a step further and notice the specific beliefs that indeed create this foundational world.

Becoming aware is the first step, and once you are aware, you can take action. When you know the specific beliefs that are limiting you from your true potential, you can create new beliefs and begin to program your subconscious mind with the version of reality you truly want, bringing you back in line with your plan and divine blueprint for your life.

Thought is not enough. Setting intentions, believing them to be true, feeling good about them, and wanting them in your reality will appear to work occasionally. But understand that attempting to create your reality with thought and feeling alone significantly limits your ability, for action is required. It is with the power of your belief, of how you perceive your world around you, combined with the action you take, that you can truly create radical and great changes in your individual and collective experience.

Great contrast has proven to motivate you and humanity to create changes. Accepting a corrupt and manipulated government has been the norm, until you collectively reach the point where change must be made. And you are nearing this now.

Change is needed in so many areas and avenues of your world. You truly can bring anything you desire into your existence, when you believe it to be possible, to be in line with you. Then your beliefs, thoughts, and feelings take on their unlimited power to create. But the core of what you experience and perceive, what manifests for you in your life, for the collective species of humanity in reality, all comes down to what you believe.

We, of course, encourage you to challenge all aspects of your reality, everything you accept and believe to be true without question; evaluate this now. Get to the core of your beliefs, and ask yourself, your body, does this really serve me? Is this belief in line with my unlimited nature? Writing down what you believe about your world and then writing a new belief, a new story of how you can create, of what you are able to accomplish, aligns you with your ultimate power as a creative being.

Tune in to your heart, to accelerate your vibration. Tune in to your heart and open to bring your physical being into alignment with the new energy, the new consciousness on earth. Be present and aware. Know that the growth and change you can create will influence the realities across the lines of time.

You are situated now at a "power point" in reality, a point in which you are unlimited, in which growth, expansion, new knowledge, ability, and human potential can rise. This is your destiny, and it also is your simple choice, between love or fear. Love motivates you, raises your energy, accelerates your vibration, and connects you to the realms of love that are present, though hidden, in your physical reality now.

Choosing love is the path of least resistance to your true intentions in your world. Yet choosing fear denies your potential, and choosing to doubt, indeed, limits your ability. Belief, trust, excitement, and love about your growth, about what you can accomplish and manifest will lead you as an individual and as a species. Love will lead you into the paradigm of heaven on earth, which has long waited to return to your planet Earth. Time, as you know it, is a very limited view.

Expand your mind, open your heart, and be fully present in this now. Breathe and be aware of your breath. Be still and calm in your now. Be present, for from this place of stillness, calm being, your power as a human being is activated.

You can begin to create and manifest anything in your world you desire. Think big, dream grand, think on a global scale and imagine your world, your life in a state of pure and total love. What does that look like, feel like?

An evolutionary shift on your planet is happening, and

you are an important part of this shift. There will be a main event, yes. But now, you can choose to integrate the spiritual energies already present on the planet. Claim your seat at the divine throne of love. Radiate love, choose love, manifest love, and love will open doors that you do not even know exist.

You have far more potential than you are aware. Release your limitations, fears, and doubts. And in your now, open your heart, raise your vibration, and move along this path of least resistance towards your highest good, towards the reunion of your physical being with your spiritual body and higher self.

You have great power to create positive change on earth. Prepare for this now and begin to use this power to create what you desire. Blessings, joy and love.

CREATING
THE NEW EARTH

Y ou are in the midst of experiencing the life of your creation. This may be hard to accept when you recognize things in life you did not want, and you think, I would never have created this—that cannot be. But know as your world gains more understanding of your reality, as science zooms in to the very atoms that make up physical objects in your realm, it can be seen, at this minute level, that creation is mostly space; not solid but empty.

Creation is creative illusion and you are here, a part of this grand illusion, this game of creating reality. First, become aware that, yes, this world is an illusion and is able to be influenced and steered in a loving way. And you are also here to empower yourself through the accelerated energies, through the energy of divine love, to create the beauty in the world that you desire.

Reality is a game and there are unlimited possibilities for how the creative energy of humanity will manifest. And at this time of great change for your world, all eyes are upon Earth. For the light you choose or choose not to experience will ripple across all realms. The change—the growth or the destruction that happens on Earth—does not stay on Earth, as it influences all levels of creation.

You are not alone in the universe. You are closely connected, woven in an intricate design of time and space, light and dark. Energies are the checkerboard of your realm, and you are here in this realm of energy to learn and expand your ability to work with energy, to claim your right as a creative being in the light, and to create in your physical world, designing your reality, manifesting the experiences, people, and situations you choose. Thoughts, feelings, and beliefs are woven together in an elaborate design.

Yet in your realm for some time now, there have been those in power who seek to control you—not to empower you to create the experience you desire, but to fit you into a neat box. You have been played to bring forth a plan, a system of control, and often chaos, scarcity, and fear. Many factors have led to this, your now experience, including the media's carefully and deliberately planted scenes of chaos, destruction, and confusion in your news, in your shows, everywhere you look in your world.

And since you are the creator of your reality, since you are creating your world, when your mind is filled with these thoughts of confusion, violence, and hatred, carefully woven and concocted into a compelling and entertaining story line, you subconsciously accept this. What you see begins to be created, and it is no wonder your world is filled with so much violence, confusion, and disruption. For these are broadcasted on all hours every day, causing those who do not choose to be empowered and create by their design, to continue to live on autopilot, unawake and unaware.

This is a dangerous combination, for those in power do not have your highest good in mind. But do not let this bother you or weigh you down because you are becoming aware of this fact and are claiming your power as the creator of your reality, observing the details of your reality. You are choosing what to focus on, what to magnetize towards you, and what to release and allow to be changed with love, by increasing your awareness, by observing and questioning, and by tuning in your now to your power within, the power of compassion, love and unity. As you recognize that all of creation is woven together intricately—not just humanity but the earth and all inhabitants upon it, the animals, the birds, the trees, the air, the water—you are one with all that is.

Begin to see your earth and your home, as you treat yourself lovingly by treating all of creation with love, gratitude, and compassion. The state of affairs on your planet earth may appear to be spiraling out of control. As species become extinct and waters polluted, it can be easy to focus on all these negatives, to worry about it, to fear it. But as you know, this draws more of it to you.

So instead, on your quest to become more aware and awakened, when you do observe these things about reality that are not in line with love, unity, and the energy of one, be aware and then choose to plant a new seed, a new thought for a more sustainable earth, a more light-filled tomorrow.

Each now moment, when you open to the energy of love, when you breathe and be in silence, stillness, and calm, you can access your infinite power inside you. With this light burning bright in your heart, illuminating all of your energy centers and your entire being, this is possible with great love, compassion, and by allowing the crystalline awareness, energy of love for your planet, into your life.

When you do this, your vibration raises to the place of peace and love, which is your birthright, and you can use these vibrations to begin to make changes in your internal world inside you. How can you be more in line with Creative Source and spirit? How can you be more loving, and joyful in your life?

We will give you a pointer, a connection to the natural world, to your living earth, and to the plants and trees, water waves, and creatures. This will bring you balance and fulfillment. As you begin to appreciate these things of your natural world in your now, you give your power to them, not to their destruction but to their growth and longevity.

There is great power in love, in your being in love, and you raise your vibration, yes. You elevate your level of experience, yes. But as you know, you are connected energetically to all humanity, and so when you evolve, you increase your awareness, expand your mind, and open your beliefs. And as a whole, as a collective species, humanity begins to shift and evolve as well. The change happens at the individual level. Great global change happens in your heart.

Do not look for your government or institutions to bring about magical changes on your earth. There has been time for this to happen, and it has not been the choice or direction. Instead of waiting for another to change your experience for the better, you are being asked to empower your life with light, love, and happiness. And by being in these emotions, you will naturally move towards attracting more light, love, and happiness. For in these emotions, you cannot consciously hurt others, hurt your planet, or be involved in the scheme of raping and pillaging your world; but you will, in the light, see your connection with all, with earth, with the Divine.

And understand on a deeper level why you are here. You are here on earth to empower yourself to become the being of light and Creative Source that you are, to use this knowledge, wisdom, and power available by tuning in to your heart. Tune in to it, your strength, and use this power to focus your intent clearly on a better tomorrow, a paradigm of love, peace and hope. And earth, as it is surrounded with a rainbow glow of light, signifying a realm of love that is safe and focused on spirit, on love, and on communion and connection with the natural world.

So many changes are needed in the physical realm now. So many eyes are watching your realm to see what will happen. What will humanity choose? Again, do not let this scare you. For ultimately your choice is fear or love. You can choose to combat with each other, to create war, and perhaps wipe yourselves out. Or you, as an individual, can choose to evolve, to increase your awareness, to become aware of the nonphysical and spiritual aspects of your world.

You can embrace your power, as a creator with the energy of love, and begin to move towards a more joyful and loving experience for yourself. As you make this choice, you do create a shift in the quantum field, a shift in the collective mind. And you are connected to all of humanities. So as you evolve, as you become more aware and present in your now, focus on manifesting heaven on earth, love as the predominant emotion on earth once again.

There is a ripple created, a ripple in time, in consciousness, in which those you are connected to also begin to become more aware and empowered. And like a great wave, this energy can carry and flow across your entire realm.

So much light is already present. At this time, it can cause challenges, as past beliefs, pain, and fear come up to be dealt with. You are being forced to feel what has been created. And when it is not according to the world you desire and design, release it, knowing that it comes up for release. And when you release past suffering, pain, doubt, and fear, you can step into love.

When you step into love, you empower your neighbor to overcome fear and embrace the now. And when your neighbor is in the now moment, in a state of love, do you see that the ripple continues? It begins with you, your open heart, and your daily communing with your divinity.

Inside you, great knowledge and wisdom are waiting to be released to create great changes in your world. But in the transitional period, it takes tuning in, quieting your mind, turning off your TV, closing your newspaper, and opening your heart to know what is happening on earth, and what is possible in your life.

When you are in love, you bring about a new paradigm of earth in love. Infinite power is in this work, your work as an awakened being on earth. Every now moment is an opportunity to move towards or away from love. Let the energy now be an opportunity for you together to move towards love, to let go of the fear, violence, and struggle of your realm, to come together with collaboration, consideration, and compassion. And with open hearts and open minds, you can experience the truth of your world, the love of your realm, and create happiness and love. And you can live in peace and balance with your natural world.

As a species, you have come so far out of line. But even this, even the current state of affairs on your world is divine. For it is probing and motivating you to change, realign, recreate, and return to love, claiming your power and creating a new earth in which all species are loved and appreciated, in which your world is respected, nurtured, and cared for, in which your physical body is seen as a glorious creation to be taken care of, honored, and developed. Your body holds great power. Open to this power through love and meditation, and through accelerating your energy by connecting with divine love.

The process is simple. Quiet your mind, relax and open your

heart. Feel love and light all around you, for it is. Breathe in. And as you breathe in life-force energy, allow it to fill your body, flowing into all spaces that may have blockages of fear or doubt. And the light you breathe in, releases these. Breathe in the light to raise your vibration, to vibrate as a spiritual being.

Open your heart to develop your psychic senses to become even more aware. Feel the love all around you and know that this love waits to be used, to be focused with intention, to manifest creative positive changes of well-being for your world. With love, anything is possible. With love, it is possible for you to fully become aware of the game you are playing here on earth. And through this awareness, you will know that your role is to radiate love, to share compassion, light and well-being with all, to love yourself, honor your path, and empower yourself to create your lifestyle by design.

Your outer world is a reflection of the beliefs, thoughts, and feelings within you. Earth, now, is a composite of these inner beliefs and feelings of all humans. Change is not something that works from the outside in. But with your internal and spiritual growth, with your returning to love in the now and focusing your intentions, backed with the power of love, on what you really want, you will see that the creation process flows from inside you to your outer world.

With inner calm, peace, and love, your outer realm will take on these characteristics as well. Love yourself enough to take the time to meditate, to quiet your mind and open your heart, to observe your natural world, to observe your beliefs and your thoughts, to refocus, recalibrate, and choose what you will experience in your life. And as you change your inner world, as you become love, light connected to the Divine, enlightened with the energy of love, your outer world will become the blissful, loving, self-sustaining, magnificent creation of divine love that it can be.

You have great power to change the natural world around you, to bring your life and life on earth back to love. Love serves you in this process, but you must focus and open your heart to allow these energies of light to manifest positive change in your world. It is happening. And with your focus now, your lifting in the vibration of love, you are infinitely powerful, loved, and on the path towards ultimate well-being.

TRANSCENDING LIMITATIONS

B e patient with yourself as you begin the process of consciously creating your reality. Self-love is the powerful force of the universe, which will keep you moving in the right direction.

There will be times when you feel you have mastered areas of creating in your realm, staying in joy, love, and peace. And then, seemingly out of nowhere, powerful and strong emotions of the contrary will be brought up. This is a normal part of the process.

Remember, as a human on earth now, you are transcending limiting beliefs from your lifetime and even those that have been stored in the collective consciousness of humanity for millennia. As these past beliefs and emotions come up for release, it is natural for you to feel down. But this is simply to draw your awareness to what needs to be released. And so, when you do find yourself feeling sad, angry, or confused for no specific reason, use your awareness to tune in, open your heart and feel.

Through your feeling guidance system, your angels are able to draw your attention and awareness towards the source of what you are feeling. Perhaps it is a belief carried through your family line, passed on to you that is now ready to go. You're not required to repeat the same steps as your parents or their parents before them.

You are a unique and powerful creative being. And as you release the old, hand the pain, suffering, and doubt over to your angels, and release it into the light each time it comes up. In doing this, you will be closer and will have an easier time of staying fully present in the light in the now.

Release the pain, the limitations, and the doubt, as they come up before you. Love yourself through the process and know it is normal for these feelings to come up. They are doing so for you to release them once and for all. This is a joyous occasion really. And so, love yourself through it to ensure you continue to move in the right direction of your ultimate manifestations, divine creations here on earth.

Another important part of the creation process is cocreating with fellow humans. The relationships you experience here in your life will bring you great joy and satisfaction, if you allow them to. These relationships can be used to manifest more of what you want. For you see, when you combine your intention with another, so that two of you are focused, excited, and moving towards the same goal, you are able to manifest this change more quickly than if you were working alone. The process of cocreation is largely what you are learning in this. Cocreating with your friends, with your family, and with the spirit, combining your intentions with the love of others, magnifies the intention and allows what you want to be drawn to you more effortlessly.

The same is true when you help others to achieve their

goals. When you assist another in bringing about a positive change in their life, even when it is completely unrelated to you and your path, the act of your helping someone else get what they want indeed creates a shift in the field.

For when you help others to get what they want, the universe in turn rewards you. The law of attraction rewards you. And when you help others to get what they want, it is natural for the manifestations, the changes you desire to experience in reality, to come true and manifest as well. Your relationships on earth are essential for your learning to manage and manipulate energy.

Becoming more aware of how you feel in the now is great. But how you feel when you are in the presence of others differs from how you feel when you are alone in a meditative state or, perhaps, even when you are just being. When you are with others, your thoughts combine with the thoughts of the other. Do you see the power? When you are both focused on your goal, on your desire, you have twice the power available for manifesting it towards you.

Love yourself through this process. Help others who come across your path to identify what they truly desire in life and to begin to move towards it. There is great power in helping others along this path. You are a way-shower. And so, when you share the knowledge and the insight you have learned that has brought you to this point, when you share your inner world with others, you are rewarded on your path as well. When you bring light, happiness, and understanding into the life of another, you cannot help but bring it into your own life.

And now on earth, in this time of great change, your ultimate purpose is to bring love, well-being, and happiness into your life. Let these emotions be your primary experience, and when you do, you will create a change in your life. As you have learned, you are connected to all. And so, when you grow and become a little more illuminated, the density of the collective mind and consciousness on earth is lightened as well. When you help a friend, even an enemy, to refocus on the light, on what they want and what they can become in this new energy, this effect is even more powerful and more pronounced in both of your lives.

Cocreate and remember the saying that is so true, "teamwork makes the dream work." When you combine forces with others in your physical reality, you are far more powerful and effective than you would be alone. Focus on the things that bring you joy, that you are good at, and the other pieces of work, the other components necessary to bring your manifestation into reality will appear.

The law of synchronicity and the law of attraction are beautiful tools. For when you are in love and when you are moving towards your goal, the universe can align the right people, the right situations, to put you in the right place at the right time, to allow all the pieces to fall into place, and to allow you to create great shifts, great change in the field of reality in which you live.

Remember that as you grow and reach a new level of being, as you master your lessons, a new lesson will appear. You are in the classroom of life, and while this is not an easy place to gain knowledge, it is oh so powerful. Each time you master a lesson, each time you are able to respond to a challenge with love, you are claiming more of your light and power. And when you are able to do this in every now moment, you will have claimed your seat in the light, as an ascended master, a light being, a leader, and a way-shower for your world.

The energies on earth are changing and shifting. As you grow, expect change to continue. It is when you allow yourself to flow with these changes, accepting them and integrating them into your life with love, that the ease and joy, which is your birthright, becomes your experience.

Challenges, strong emotions, sadness, signal that there is still learning for you. In the moment, when you are in these emotions, feel them, tune in to them. Find the location in your body where they are stored cellularly by tuning in, by feeling. What is this tied to? Is it from this life, a past life? Is it someone else's emotion that you are tuning in to?

Be aware. Be ever more aware of how you are feeling, of what it is that you're feeling, and where these feelings come from. When you do, you can release those that no longer serve you. You can choose to focus again on your intention, on what you really want, on helping others, loving yourself, being positive, being in love, surrounding yourself in light.

Each time you return to this space in the now, you are empowered. Each time you consciously choose to define and create your experience, you are empowering yourself. The now moment is the source of your power. Your power is ready to be claimed. You deserve this control. You deserve goodness, love, and well-being in your life. And this is truly possible when you open to love, when you love yourself, move towards your goals, help others to get what they want, and return to love, evermore time and time again in your now.

Love is the power that moves you forward towards full empowerment—being aware and observant, raising your vibration, and accelerating your energy—which is your path to mastering your role as an active creator in physical reality.

You are a spiritual being and your power is vast. With love, compassion, and understanding, you are able to integrate these innate abilities. Open to new powers, new strengths, and lead the way for a balanced humanity on earth in peace and love.

YOUR
HAPPINESS
ADVANTAGE

Y ou have an internal guidance system that allows you to know if you are headed in the direction of your ultimate goal. Your guidance system helps you to determine if you are moving towards or away from your soul purpose.

How does this guidance system operate? Through joy. You see, joy is the most powerful vibration you can embody to align with what you want. Furthermore, you are innately designed to enjoy those things that will bring you the most reward, fulfillment, and growth as a spiritual being here on earth.

The activities aligned with your true purpose will feel fun, bring excitement, evoke passion, and increase happiness in your life. And so, if you find you are not enjoying your work or your day-to-day activities, you are receiving powerful soul feedback from your authentic self to get back into a state of joy. If you are not doing what you really want to be doing, we ask you why you are doing it.

You are not required on this earth to follow the dreams or aspirations of another. And yet, so many humans do indeed choose to chase after goals, dreams, and ideals that have nothing to do with why they are truly here. When this happens, the activities and work are draining and are not fulfilling or fun. If you are in this sort of situation now, take time to reconnect and re-identify with the things that do bring you joy.

Your interests and the passions that drive, motivate, and excite you are the very things that will keep your body healthy, in tune, and allow you to live a long healthy and happy life.

Joy keeps your internal organs functioning with ease. Joy aligns you with harmonious relationships, and then together, you can send more happiness, joy, and light out into your world, cocreating more of what you ultimately desire. Joy holds great power in your relationships to draw you together and ensure a lasting and fulfilling balance. Joy is your path of least resistance.

When you are in joy, the events, people, situations required to bring about what you really want will effortlessly fall into place. Joy is the path of least resistance. You are able to feel excitement, passion, and happiness about your work, your hobbies, and really about your life. And you can be certain that the laws of your universe will work to align, to bring you more to be joyful about when joy is a foundation for your experience.

And so we encourage you to be in love and in joy—not for our well-being but to bring about what you have truly desired to create here in the physical. You are alive in your body with your personality and your unique energy signature, which will never again be the same. This is not your only life, but it is the only now in which you are you, in which your present personality is vibrant and ready to bring about blessings, changes, manifestations on earth.

Follow the trail of happiness to align with your true purpose. If you're not happy or not feeling good, it's likely that your thoughts, your actions, and the world you are creating is out of line with the true, deep inner desires and the authentic knowing of your soul.

So the answer is simple. Let happiness be your advantage. Let happiness propel you forward in the right direction. If you bounce through life from happy event to happy event, from positive encounter to joyful experience, you can be sure you are moving in the right direction and are expanding and ascending.

Joy and love are your birthright. And when you are in these beautiful and positive emotions, you are in the right place at the right time. You are taking the right steps towards your goals. As you continue to allow joy and love to lead the way in your life, new developments, exciting coincidences, and truly anything is possible with the power of love and happiness on your side. Cultivate these emotions in you. Affirm that you are happy and loved and that these emotions are your primary response to all of life's situations.

There are no easy lessons in life's journey, and you are often asked to deal with what is most difficult for you. But this does not mean that struggle is required. By aligning with joy, you can learn your life's lessons with grace, ease, and happiness, and continue forward with a positive trajectory.

This, of course, will bring you fulfillment and happiness because these are the very emotions that will lead you towards accomplishing your true purpose.

Let happiness be your guide. And through this subtle shift in your perspective, you can choose to be happy always, even when things are not going exactly as you had planned or hoped, even when your job or present situation is less than ideal. Being in joy in your now will bring you back into alignment even if you have gotten far off your true path.

The power of joy can transform every aspect of your life. Let this vibration work through you. Let yourself be happy, and choose experiences that make you happy. Move towards goals that bring you happiness. Let happiness be your objective, and all other desires will align with this central focus.

Follow joy and the universe will provide you with all you need to remain in positivity, happiness, and love. Your role in reuniting your physical realm completely with the higher realms, with the vibrations of happiness, joy, and love, is to simply choose these experiences for yourself.

Commit to loving yourself, to being happy, to following your inner promptings, desires, and dreams—not living your life for another but understanding that although you are connected to all individuals, you are responsible for your own experience. There are so many blessings for you when you step into your power, rather than remaining on autopilot and continuing to let others choose your reality.

Claim your empowerment now. This time is all about your ever-expanding awareness and claiming your seat as conscious creator of your reality. And for this to work, for you to create what you desire deep inside your heart, begin to observe yourself from a third person perspective and notice the triggers that cause you to slip away from the love, happiness, and well-being that actually lead you towards your goal.

When you encounter one of these triggers, it is actually a great blessing because it can be addressed once and for all. Change how you respond to your world. When you find yourself sending anger or sadness, know why and realize it is a choice. And regardless of what has happened in your life, you can choose right now to love, to experience well-being, happiness, contentment, and peace.

You have the power to consciously choose how to respond in the moment and how you feel. Choose to feel good in your now and you will consistently be drawing to you experiences, realities, people, and opportunities that will move you further along your path in joy, love, and well-being.

The choice is yours. Know that each time you choose to respond with happiness, you lay the foundation so your next happiness choice will be a little easier and more automatic, until finally, love, happiness, and joy are your automatic reactions.

This change in you ripples out across the lines of time, bringing happiness, healing, and love to all of your experience, past, present, and future. There is great power for you to affect all levels of reality from within this present moment. Use your now moment wisely by feeling, being, and radiating happiness, joy, and love.

THE POWER
OF LOVE

G reat love, peace and joy is indeed possible as your birthright, and this will come to be your primary experience of reality when you are able to send and receive love in every now.

The turbulence of your world may present you with situations for drama, challenges, and tests to see where you are on your path and to gauge your level of mastery. Life lessons and tests, which assess your ability to choose love in the moment, to see through illusion and chaos, and help you to see things as they actually are—Divine, one, whole. Yes, you indeed are able to fully embrace this perspective by detaching yourself from the drama, trusting in the process, and allowing yourself to love, especially when it is challenging and the events of the world urge you to respond otherwise.

When you are able to love at all, you are claiming your role as a way-shower within your ascending world. Plus, the changes, dreams, and manifestations you desire in your life, physical and nonphysical, are all possible with love.

Sharing love opens you to receive more. It is through the sending and receiving of love that your experience truly begins to take shape. And by simply staying in gratitude, hope, and peace, in vibrations that resonate with love, you can be assured you are moving in line on your divine path of love.

The love you give to another does not exit your life and enter theirs. But rather, all love you send out comes back to you multiplied. When you do bring joy and love into the life of another, and it then inspires them to be more loving and treat others with kindness and happiness, you can see the ripple effect in action. What you cannot fully see is the love you give to another, that they give to another, is then passed on to another. The huge impact of this entire love ripple returns all of the compounding energy to you. Increased love allows you to elevate to your next level of becoming, stepping into your next level of being present in love.

Be present in this very moment right now and honor, remember, and consider that you are indeed connected to the entire world around you; you are one with all. Be aware that divine love exists in everyone and everything on your planet, including you, and that you and all are divine. Recognizing this will help empower you to make the choices that honor and nurture others and yourself, which empowers you to release perceived negativity and to fully enter, embrace, and surround yourself with love.

Imagine this now. What does it feel like to be completely surrounded with love?

You are surrounded now with golden energy and the light of divine love—love energy, peace, and warmth. Breathe in as love fills your body; lift, float, and allow it to raise your vibration. Allow yourself to become illuminated and filled with the energy of love now. As it washes over you and through you, close your eyes, breathe, feel, and visualize love all around you creating a protective shield, illuminating, lightening, and cleansing.

As you fill yourself with love and light to this degree, there may be lower vibrations that come up, which do not resonate in these higher vibrations. If or when this happens, love these feelings too, honor their place, and release them into the light, so you can more fully resonate love.

Now with help from your guides, allow your memory to draw your awareness to someone in your life whom you have consciously or unconsciously hurt, wrongly judged, or perhaps said things you did not mean. Allow this person or situation to come into your awareness, knowing that you are filled with love. And now let your love surround this person, as you send it out from your heart to heal and restore. And yes, the love you send out benefits this one. But it also now flows back to you multiplied, cleansed, and elevated.

You are in the process of becoming fully accountable as a creator within your world. To do this, you must open fully to your power, your light, and your creative ability. Love guides you through this, shows you your way, and enables you to create great change on a global scale. Love allows humanity to overcome the manipulation, power, and control present on earth for centuries, and to fully enter into the new paradigm of peace, hopes and wishes for a better tomorrow. Your intention, your dream, your love truly allows this better tomorrow to be.

Release the mainstream media images of war and tragedy, doubt and fear. Surround yourself with positive people and affirmations, pictures of what you want, and visions of a better tomorrow.

Imagine how great, beautiful, and love filled your life can truly be. And with your imagination, your desire, your inner prompting, the creative process begins. Creation takes form around you. Stay in love to lead the way for your species to live in balance, in unity as one. By living in love and responding with love, the struggles and challenges you face will be easily overcome.

Love is a powerful ally for attaining anything you truly desire. Trust. Believe in the power of love. Take time to quiet your mind, release your fears, and open your heart to radiate as the spiritual loving being you are. Through this, you create your vision of heaven on earth, of a peaceful loving reality.

Create the new paradigm of earth now with love. All that you need is available to you now—the inner knowledge, wisdom, truth, and inner power. Align yourself with your higher self, the spiritual you that is fully connected and powerful, fully light.

Let this power manifest through you in your realm. Stand up, be bold, and love beyond the illusion to truly bring what you want into manifestation. It is possible. Unlimited potential in love awaits.

Get into the flow of creation by allowing love into your life, by sharing love with others, and by responding with love in every now. Do this and you will become who you are destined to be: a spiritual and love-filled being of light, peace and truth.

We leave you with our blessing. Know that, indeed, the light burns bright in you; but nurture it, honor it to allow it to grow, to claim this creative control, to live your life by your design.

CREATING
WITH CHRIST
LIGHT

The light in you, Christ consciousness, divine love, the second coming—much prophecy and focus in your realm has been on this future date, the second coming of the messianic Christ.

And we say to you, the time in which you live is now. You live in the time of the return of the Christ light. But know that this light is not some external being. This light lives in you and in all.

Your world is now experiencing a great influx of cosmic energy—accelerating the field and everything within from intense frequency bursts that radiate from the center of your galaxy, accelerating your realm and pushing you to fully connect with your light, your spirit, and with Christ consciousness within you.

The return of Christ does not speak of one man but is about the evolution of humanity as a whole. As you enter the new age, embracing the spirit and light within you,

you are able to access the field that Christ tuned in to of miracles, manifestation, and unconditional love.

As energy pours into the earth from the cosmos, the stars, and your sun, you are given the opportunity repeatedly to develop your psychic and spiritual abilities. And the more you effectively focus on this, the more profound the results you will achieve.

Ultimately, to fully open to this light, to Christ consciousness, to your spiritual body and your full awareness—fully awakened, fully tuned in to your multidimensional and spiritual self—all you must do is remain focused on love to let the truth of love define you and your life. Let love flow in and all around.

In contrast, fear is a long-standing belief here in the physical realm broadcast by media and focused on by all at some point. And the accelerated energy, the crystalline light pouring into earth, offers you opportunity in every now to let go of all your fears, to surrender the dense, chaotic fears of the past and let them go. Like holding and then dropping a pen, so too can you release the fear and focus on love within your heart.

Choose to respond with compassion towards others. Choose to treat yourself with love. And through this powerful emotion and energy vibration, the light within you becomes bright, and the Christ light awakens Christ consciousness present on earth within all. When you choose love, when you choose to open your heart, you effectively choose to tune in to your Christ consciousness, to your ability to perceive reality beyond the physical and in the realm of love.

You see, reality is very much filled with illusion, and yet you are able to create within this realm. With your Christ light burning bright, with love leading and guiding you through your life and down your divine path, you truly have an unlimited ability to manifest positive change, blessings, miracles, and love in your world—the same love and healing that Christ was able to channel into the world.

You too can access divine teaching, wisdom, and love. You too can nurture your spirit, honor your soul, and tune in to the love and light from within your heart. Feel the divine love all around you, and let this into your being. Let the cosmic energies from the center of the galaxy enter into your experience by letting go of fear, quieting your mind, and allowing your heart to open your awareness to expand.

Lift up and breathe in to the spiritual being you are becoming, a light being divinely inspired. You are able to affect the field, to manifest your desires and blessings, to create love as the Christ consciousness awakens more and more, thanks to this flow of accelerated energy.

You have the ability to bring about great and lasting changes, empowering more of humanity to awaken, to recognize the illusion, the message of fear and the chaos portrayed by media, and to realize you can choose your own truth. You can know when stories are concocted creatively to manipulate and spread more fear.

Whenever you come across a situation in your world where you fear, recognize that illusion is present and, with your bright shining light, you are not threatened but you are safe. And responding to the trigger and the events around you with love, enables your light to burn even brighter.

The masters who have come before you, the Christ, Buddha, Kuan Yin, and others, all had one thing in common: the ability to return to love in the now, time and time again. Self-love, love for all, love for the Divine, love brightly shining in you activates your DNA to your full potential, awakens you to your spiritual body, your spiritual energy, your multidimensional self. It enables you to heal yourself, your earth, your family, and to bring light, to shine light to heal across the lines of time.

By simply choosing in this now, balance, peace, and love, those choices ripple out across the web of interconnectedness, creating positive change in the past for your ancestors, your parents, your children, and for all. The growth you individually experience does not end with you. It ripples out and creates continued change enabling you to make a difference in the life of another.

As you awaken even more yourself, then those who are still asleep to their inner divine light, submerged in the illusion, they too will begin to awaken to inner light, inner power, connection with spirit, source, and love. This powerful combination truly allows you to bring blessings into your realm, to redefine your beliefs about your reality, and to quickly change the way you perceive, experience, and manifest in your world—to fully open to your Christ consciousness, to your full spiritual light, spiritual nature, divinity.

Choose love in your now. Let go of fears and limiting thoughts. Open your heart. Share love, compassion, and joy with all you encounter. Realize you are a physical being here, yes, but you are spirit. And this spirit that you can tap into and flow through your body holds divine intelligence, knowledge and wisdom to guide you in your life.

The chaos and struggle of this earthly realm are no longer needed. The great blessing of this transition, of this ascension and the accelerated energy is that you are able to leave behind the limitations, to open to your full ability in the light, to the full awareness and knowing that you are a divine being.

This is not exaggerated, cocky, or aiming too high, but it is the next step in human evolution: mind, body, and spirit united as one, united in love. With this alignment, you will know your truth that you came here to create. You will know your full path, one step at a time.

Take your next step. Share your light and love with one another. Know that as your light, your Christ consciousness burns brighter, you encourage others to awaken and activate their divine potential as well. You are all interconnected. You are one.

Indeed, the growth, the love, and the light you open to does not end with your experience. It is connected to all. And so, your growth, your transmuting fear and choosing love, allows increased love to take form in your realm, to take over for fear, chaos, and doubt. This will let the earth, once again, return to the joyous, peaceful, and loving center it is becoming.

Your role is to open, trust, surrender, and allow the divine energies to flow through you. Awaken from slumber. Create your world by design.

GRATITUDE
FOR ALL

- Gratitude for all the people and spiritual beings who collectively helped to create this book.

- Gratitude for all who read these words.

- Gratitude for all that has been and all that will be.

- Gratitude for all the opportunities to learn, love, and grow.

- Gratitude for all of life.

- Gratitude for all that is.

Free .MP3
Angel Message

To experience a channeled audio meditation by Melanie, download your free .mp3 Angel Message here!

www.Ask-Angels.com/love

ABOUT THE AUTHOR

M elanie Beckler is an internationally acclaimed author, spiritual teacher, and clear channel of the light.

Through walking the path of an open heart, Melanie has remembered her direct link with the Divine and angelic realms. She feels both honored and blessed to share the ever-unfolding and expanding guidance, love, and uplifting energy that flow through as a result of her direct connection with the realm of angels.

Melanie remains focused on publishing the empowering teachings from spirit to assist humanity and earth in the ascension process.

For more information visit: **www.Ask-Angels.com**

Connect with Melanie on Social Media

Facebook: **facebook.com/askangelsfan**

YouTube: **youtube.com/askangels**

Twitter: **twitter.com/askangels**

Instagram: **instagram.com/askangels**

9786984R00076

Printed in Germany
by Amazon Distribution
GmbH, Leipzig